The Phoenix Living Poets

ON THE WAY TO THE DEPOT

The Phoenix Living Poets

MEASURES
A ROUND OF APPLAUSE
A COMMON GRACE
SURROUNDINGS
Norman MacCaig

THIS COLD UNIVERSE
THE WORLD I SEE
Patric Dickinson

ADDICTIONS
SOME MEN ARE BROTHERS
THE OLD ADAM
D. J. Enright

WHEN THAT APRIL
Gillian Stoneham

POEMS
Lotte Zurndorfer

TIME FOR SALE
Edward Lowbury

SELECTED POEMS
James Merrill

THE SUN MY MONUMENT
Laurie Lee

FAIRGROUND MUSIC
John Fuller

THE RE-ORDERING OF THE STONES
NATURE WITH MAN
Jon Silkin

CONTROL TOWER
Richard Kell

THE SWANS OF BERWICK
Sydney Tremayne

WORDS FOR BLODWEN
Gloria Evans Davies

POEMS
Alexander Baird

THE DIRECTIONS OF MEMORY
Laurence Lerner

SELECTED POEMS
Robert Pack

THE YEAR OF THE WHALE
George Mackay Brown

THE BURNING HARE
J. C. Hall

MEN WITHOUT EVENINGS
David Gill

ON THE WAY
TO THE DEPOT

by

P. J. KAVANAGH

CHATTO AND WINDUS

THE HOGARTH PRESS

1967

Published by
Chatto and Windus Ltd
with the Hogarth Press Ltd
42 William IV Street
London WC2

★

Clarke, Irwin and Co Ltd
Toronto

Printed in Great Britain by
T. H. Brickell and Son Ltd
The Blackmore Press, Gillingham, Dorset

Contents

FOR SALLY

Saint Tropez

Cast off in a boat without even a head for companion
You washed up here and I must say they gave you a welcome:
Renamed their gulf and their village and every so often
Fire guns at the ground in your honour.
You couldn't have known you'd so noisily float to the future
When someone in Pisa repeated
The claims of a dim jewish mystagogue thirty years hanged:
So what made you refuse to deny them
When Nero your master requested and thereby lose your head?
Those who back the wrong cult have to do without bangs
On their nameday. And it's hard, surely,
To lay down your neck for a long-shot, all alone?

Well, now you've a life-size painted porcelain portrait
Complete with moustache (a chocolate-coloured d'Artagnan)
A trellis of red paper flowers and, every day, roses.
An unthrifty aureole, even, of high-watt bulbs
Burns all day and night in the dark of your church.
Today the obedient carry your head in procession.

Teach us, Signore, to love a good thing when we see one:
Also the perfect moment to disobey.

May 16th 1962

Dominus illuminatio mea

Ah! What creeping of late-summer shadows from the yew
    trees
Rooks' restlessness and evening gramophones . . .

We sped (you're as young as you feel)
From London in the roadster,
Opened the borrowed cottage, had us a fry-up,
Tossed a coin for the four-poster bedroom
And went to our separate dreams.

What a wonderful thing is male friendship!
You, planning a sure domestic murder
(Sexual freedom is an onerous thing
But love love love ah! love is King!)
I, (old friend of you both) required to lend
A confiding, tolerant ear for the week-end.
And now we're waiting for the pubs to open
Reading the Sunday papers in Trinity garden.
Spiked in the wall-top mortar, coldly, like emeralds, glow
Hand-slicing broken bottles drunk two centuries ago.

O barbered walks leading to bird-perch statues –
I follow where you lead!
Newman's head startles, impaled on a plinth,
As though he'd been executed and dipped in green.

The college cat
Is contentedly playing with something on the grass:
The squeak of living bones, alas! carries the distance.
Surely it's nearly seven!

Bartok is ribboning over a sill chipped clean
In the nick of its crumble away.
For a new generation?
Where will they put them all? Where will they put the
        cripples?
But we live, after all, and this was a place,
A week-end, good as another to miss the point in.

Lines for my father

Methods of dodging are as many
As kinds of emptiness, and you were master
Of every kind and method.
Once in a decade unwillingly
Trapped in no laughing matter
You were curiously tender;
Otherwise brisk, and plump with contradictions:
Able to pray, even think, like a bigot, you'd argue
Some poor priest's ears red;
At times of partings you slipped away so aptly
To seek out crowds, as though they hid salvation;
A faithful, beloved husband, often drunk.
There seemed such strength of emotion in your evasions!
Above all there were jokes, and yours were good ones,
Indeed they fed and clothed us, paid my school.
Were you happy ever? Do you still snort at such questions?
When you stared at the wall when you died, what did you see?

Plain tale from the hills

They didn't like the colour of our skins
(not having time to discover our sympathies).
What the hell? We'd other sins
we'd got away with. There's a kind of justice.

Surprising, their hostility, how it shaped our lives.
Bien pensants, we were forced behind barbed-wire
which kept them out and us, effectively, in:
with Oil executives (the Firm sent home their wives)
who paid for quick release behind the Club
and called the girls black monkeys as they wiped their flies.

Frogs at night in the garden were the sound
of iron hooves in a courtyard echoing round and round;
the elastic snap of a tree-snake spoiled our noon.
If we opened the window (sick of the air-conditioner)
we let in the soft night-time murmur
from the squatters' leaf-huts, which shouldn't have been there
anyway, spoiling the avenue.

But we doted on Rex the Alsatian with his soft brown eyes,
gentle, affectionate – yes, old Rex was loyal! –
trained to go for the throat of any intruder.
And we loved the old house-boy till sensing a change of order
he started to keep the money on the empties.
Mildly rebuked for this (servants were scarcer)
being unused to dishonour, and confused,
he went to the master-bedroom, sat on the bed and slipped his
knife in his groin and pulled it up to his navel.
It was Rex's whimpers of pleasure attracted us,
lapping the blood that trickled down the hall.

The spring

(Korea)

The paper house was empty in the middle of the paddy
So we took it over. The electricians
Fixed up some wiring; we had a crate of
Guinness in the lorry; we'd come a long way
But first we must get settled.
The partitions, the rooms, were small. The locals were
    small,
But the owner must have been a man of some substance,
There were plenty of rooms, and the house miles from
    nowhere.
Soon there were yellow bulbs swinging from black flex;
All had their quarters; a dry-patch for the lorries . . .
Then somebody smelled the burning.
Something wrong with the wiring.
Up to our anklets in mud
We watched it burn down, drinking Guinness.
Nothing for it now but put up tents on the dry-patch.
A man floated face downward in the mud.
There were helmets and webbing equipment we didn't
Inquire under. Now there was kerosene
In the tents, and wooden duck-walks.

In front of the smouldering house,
In the shallow pond where the man lay,
Was a bubble of spring; in the morning
We went there to wash. It was warm.
Out of the earth, dribbling on to the mud
Between two stones, came a spring that was warm.
We used it to shave in; while around,
Women patiently gathered with their washing:
The people whose blessing it was
Waiting for us to go.

August by the river

Hunched-up, muttering along the *quais*
Of deserted, bus-ticket-blown SW3,
After one too many a *table d'hôte* meal
Eaten alone with a book, I think of Jules
Laforgue. As I zig-zag along beside
The only river that openly solicits suicide,
I think of St. Barnabas, Addison Road,
Only a couple of postal districts away
Where, oddly enough, he married a Miss Leah Lee.
With my pockets stuffed full like confetti with telephone
Numbers I'll never ring up, I stop to stare the moon
Over Battersea full in its diesel-fumed eye,
For I'm terrified stiff of the quiet in my *chambre meublée.*
Why do I think of Jules Laforgue and his bride?
Because by this stretch of the river, whose arms
Offer their piss-yellow, typhus-ridden charms –
Because it's probably wiser and safer in this *quartier*
To think of them and not of you, or me.

Watch this space

When they placed in position de Witter's 'Adam and Eve'
On the front of the Marriage Counsel Office block –
Two low-relief panels with a space between,
Two oblong verticals, asymmetrical – the shock
They gave us was (presumably)
Something to do with his cock
And her petals. Both showed, certainly.
But even after they'd been taken down
And his knocked off and hers smoothed in
Their modified presences still disturbed our town.
What is it about them? We don't believe
In this of course, but isn't it odd
That in the uncarved space between the figures, some god,
Some kind of superstition appears to stand
Guarding a silence with an empty hand?

Wherever you are

Dropped fully grown, conceived by autogenesis,
My smiling devils are gaolers who simulate friendliness
The better to break me. They thrive in the semi-awake
Of the utterly dark of their birth-place. One, arm around my
    neck,
Explaining why I keep my curtains drawn:
"Why bother to open them? When you look down
I am all the faces of the town.
Be honest now: when did you last see a different one?"
His birth and his chatter exhaust me. For peace I lie down and
    confess
My god is theirs whose name is nothingness.

But in our darkness the warm-lipped angels also have their
    places,
More terrible by far,
Whose wings are wands of anamnesis,
More than flesh and blood and brain can bear.
My devils are easier, teaching forgetfulness!
But if I turn away
From these insupportable angels of memory
I pull a blind of horror between me
And the natural world: pig-snout and bird-claw instead of
    hands and faces.

You must save me angels! Tell me what to do!
"Action is all the meaning left you now.
Lift up your back from the bed,
Strain till the sweat is running down your head
To repeat like a parrot what we tell you to say:
I believe in you, angels. Devils, you lie."

And now on the screen of myself, in the dark I can see
Each watchful face that, hurt, like all ours are,
Opened like a child's face, like a flower,
While it was looking at her.

Theirs than hers are easier to remember.

Quickly now . . . what phrases can I mutter,
Having reached this far, to weave them like a charm
Round the legs of my bed
Before the dark in me begins to swarm
And puts out all the daylight from my head?
How sweeten my tongue? How summon the flavour of her?

Now, as prisoners rotting in the black
Of forgotten dungeons pick from stinking straw
Their half-dry faeces, using them as chalks to draw
Crucifixions, a flower, a beloved name, in the dark,
So I use this, my day-long, night-long back-
And-forth to scratch your name with.
                                        You, the law
I live by, in the dark. You, the tenement
By rarest, luckiest accident,
Of more than you knew, more than your mirror saw.

And so in the dark I talk to you out loud.
I no longer know if I talk to you or God.

And what have you to do with prisoners and darkness,
Black and white angels, metaphors of pain,
Whose soul was so strong it retained that initial, mysterious
        happiness
The rest of us lose at once, and never have again?
You are the silence I listen to,
The landscape of the dark I move through –

And none of these things—
                    the dark is mine
And yours and ours – oh help me see
How all the angels in the darkness can agree
That nothing I have, not even my pain is my own:
That under an absence like a stone, I must be gay!

Westwell, Oxfordshire

Sky mother-of-pearl. Oyster-colour sun
A furry lemon,
Silent, full of silences.
Birdless windless trees hold breath;
Stream tinkles to pond to be frozen to death.
Silence: a hand clapped over a mouth;
Violent, with suppressed violences.
Earth is preoccupied, waiting to know
The soft grope of snow.
Muscles of a bough crack, pistol-shot, echo echo . . .
On a little mound
Near stream, by pond,
A church: a square of yellow stone,
Some of it ferried over seas from Caen
In boats too light, you would have thought,
To bear the weight,
Ages of faith ago.
Moss on the church-yard gate.
Green grass prickles the hoar-frost sheet.
And then the moment like a film-shot freezes.
Perceived, not seen, almost out of frame:
Joy. A presence,
Transforming all the other presences:
And leaning against a new-cut yellow stone
A splash of carmine
A scatter of frozen
Bokhara roses . . .
And then the blur of snow. Time to be gone.

Sequence

New Year's morning
> I didn't love you, you didn't love me,
> You stayed for no reason but soft attraction
> And snow on the road to North London.
> You were large and beautiful and jewish
> and very warm. We slept
> unsatisfied each, and quite content.
> And when in the morning you stood in the light
> slowly to strap your daytime on
> was born in me the power to love again.
> Simple as that.
> And you, thank God in love with somebody else
> (such moments are not rushed upon so soon)
> laughed in the mirror with wonder – Look
> I've last year's make-up on!
> And you were gone.

January
> Beauty's a flame
> draws us on and on.
> A candle inside a hollow, sculpted head.
> Huddled head to head
> we kept our mysteries all afternoon.
> No one is anything now. If you leave
> collapsed on my table, your hand's covering, your glove,
> empty of fingers, full of bought fragrance – if I move
> to hold it for a moment to my face
> I know I yearn
> not wholly for you:
> but once again
> according to the law we serve
> I want to burn.

February

Leaning on Waterloo Bridge after ninety days
of dark and snow and sludge in sudden sun:
there are black-headed gulls all round *Discovery*;
there's Blackfriars and Westminster and out-of-sight
       Lambeth
and concave pencilling skyscraping Vickers
(unfinished) and altogether a sense of bank-to-bankness,
of being near a river in a city.
Buying an evening paper at two o'clock
among the girlie books the breasts
and buttocks and (curious taste) suspenders,
I blame myself for being so lost in myself
I have to remember the miracle blue of the sky
and to bless the man who coloured buses red.
(There are still the letters PLEASURE GARDEN
clinging to a mass of cemented rubble).
I'd like to palp the typists as they pass.
For I am happy.
What else can you be when two
enormous out-of-scale hetaerae hold up
the portico of a station called Waterloo?

April

I have a fear we shall quarrel
when we are alone.
You, opiniated, foolish, beautiful,
who all the virtues own
of the over-demanding, over-fastidious mind.
Who live without a friend
save the man you love, and me.
How shall the red fox, flushed from the roots of his tree,
wagging his red brush, playing at dog,
nose tender with hedgehog,
and you, lover of uncornered foxes, ever agree?
Well, says the red fox, wait; wait and see.

20

June

Phrases out of a letter:
'Running elbow to elbow with the President's brother
in the three-legged race his long-legged daughters
had huge, dark eyes.'
Does it matter?
So many girls in the world.
Who will bother?
Stripped, heads shaven, one in line with the other,
could we, as a uniformed guard, three weeks after
going on oven-duty
guarantee
even to raise a flicker?

My hands hang down, stream blood.
I cannot distinguish.
The crowd
is over me like a hood of blood.

On the plate of a body bearing a head
someone has carried this letter, watches me read it.
Odd
to distinguish a head in Horrible Town
and it still on.

Now I'm a bird and looking down:
white distempered in a believable sun
a place for people
is built on Horrible Town;
almost
almost bearing it down.

September

Cold light of the moon, over the sleeping sea,
over the whale-back islands, over me
here in a cottage on the mountain's hip,
capture me, asleep.
Drag my memories through your freezing streams
until they're come out cold and hard as stones
I can hold in my hand:
stones I can build with,
the dreams and memories my waking days are filled with.
I want a stone tower made of them in my mind;
one I can climb, and signal from, and understand.

On the way to the depot

It's a pleasant night. So tonight I'll talk on the way
Of the images I seem to think in every day
Five strange years after:
Of how my life appears to me.
I don't speak of it, the thing itself, not that,
But of how I seem to see our lives in the light of it.
It's as though you live in big rooms filled with laughing;
I see little tables, and shining black pianos,
And you very busy. And me outside in the street
(Don't laugh) sweeping it.
The place I suppose is my idea of heaven.
I haven't described it (who could?)
But I've put in some writing desks and black pianos
Because that's if I'm honest, the best my poor brain can rise to
Without inventing. Spirits, like flames that meet
Melting into each other – yes, that makes sense to me often
But not (and you know this) every day...
Anyway, here I am
Out on the pavement. And every night
I wheel my day's collection to the depot
Where it's assessed. But
(And here's the odd part)
I don't know who does the assessing
Or what it's best to bring. One just leaves it all there
And goes to bed; every day.
The streets and dreams and faces that I've seen now
Without you. Or with you?
  It's late.
Time to turn in my collection.
Heaven knows how I'm doing!
When I sleep
Visit me then, reassure me. Don't share my puzzle.
And let me hear you laugh at my dustman's hat. . . .

Afternoon in Sneem

At three o'clock on the green
a Vauxhall stops and out of the boot
in a resonant unaccompanied baritone comes
Christ crucified for me.
None of the lips move of the men who are in it.
The fairground men from Ballylongford
lean on their hammers;
children out of school, their plastic sandals
hanging in their fingers, wait to listen;
and the men under the eaves
or inside M. J. O'Sullivan's, Riney's, P. J. Burns',
their hillsides left to the wet,
stare at their boot-toes.
"We are not Jehovah Witnesses."
Boot-lid lifted, tape-recorder switched
to crowd-speaker, a pale, stout young man
in a broad tie and a tie-clip: "We disagree
with all their teachings."

"They're Jehovah's Witnesses." Huge hat tipped back,
the village doctor, venal sheriff out of a Western,
loudly pronounces. "They all believe
they're saved. It comes from America."
"That sounds easy" says the friendly visitor.
"I find *my* religion easy." Chin thrust out;
uncontradicted, champion of the Church, rolls to the pub next
        door.
The pints all sigh, relax their gaze
fixed over glass-brim, nowhere.
"There's nothing wrong in what they're saying"
whispers a cap, "they're Christians anyway."

Old Jack Mountain, half in half out,
his ears holding his hat up, is caught.
"Are you saved?"
                    "We'll see now."
"Then don't you trust in the Lord?"
"Now I never said that."
"Good theology" nods a listening trilby.

Outside the rain is falling in hatfuls.
Dowager Winnie behind the bar
absently dusts a loaf, rolls up some twine,
combs the froth off the stout-jug
and peers through her peephole across the empty green.
The Ballylongford men are taking their ease in doorways –
*Dance till ten to the Fabulous Des O'Donovan and his Five
Sisters (Galway)* – their half-up Bingo tent is sagging water,
peeling roundabout horses tilt in mud.
"I read in a book" comes from the empties corner
"written in America,
that weather will make this country
unfit for habitation." Takes a sip:
"They didn't put a date on it."
"Trouble was" (Jack, judicially, over a second)
"I never had a long enough read at the Bible."

Outside on the green in the Vauxhall the four city-men
pent in by bruise-coloured mountains,
sit staring in silence before them
their windows slowly misting in the rain.

The Temperance Billiards Rooms

The Temperance Billiards Rooms in red and green and brown
with porridge-coloured stucco in between
and half a child's top for a dome, also green –
it's like a Protestant mosque! It'll come down;
no room for this on the Supermarket scene.
Eight years ago on a Saturday afternoon
we used to walk past it, for no particular reason,
dressed in our weekend clothes now long out of fashion,
and bump into friends, newly married, just as we were,
and go to a film, or not, or window-shop.
Eight years before that I was seventeen,
eight years from now I may be forty-one;
thirty-three salutes the Billiards Rooms alone.
Because I'm the one who's alive still, but without much
        enthusiasm,
for loving someone has no particular season,
just goes on, as I do too I notice; not only from fear –
though it's true I don't want to go for I've never been there –
but while you are breathing it takes a decision to stop;
and I'm vaguely pleased to see that green and brown
(something so uneconomical's sure to come down)
in all its uselessness waiting out its season:
pleased to find the Temperance Billiards Rooms still here,
and for all I know men playing billiards temperately in there.

In the rubber dinghy

In the rubber dinghy on the lake
watched from the bank I secretly touched your leg
when I should have been watching you.
You were pleased but it was the wrong thing to do.
I was afraid and it was a trick
like watching a star askew;
stare straight at it and you miss the glow.
I protected myself and I protected you.
We touched as lovers do
pretending to paddle the boat on the little lake
when my whole life was burning for your sake;
watched from the bank by others whose treasure you were
but who didn't love you as I did and could stare
safely straight at you and marvel at what they saw.
You were mine because you'd decided so.
For safety I did as other lovers do
when that wasn't what was needed then. No.
We could have fallen together into the glow
that was waiting. I wanted a slow
lifetime for that and looked askew.
So we were simply happy and laughed on the lake
and I have a lifetime to think out my mistake.

Perfection isn't like a perfect story

I think often of the time I was perfectly happy.
And sat by the harbour reading a borrowed Cavafy.
You were with me of course and the night before we
Played bar billiards, green under lights, in the café
Postponing our first shared bedtime and every ball
That didn't come back made us look at each other and down.
I collected the key and we crossed the late-night hall
And seeing the room you cried, it was so small.

We were too close. We bore each other down.
I changed the room and we found that you were ill.
Nothing was perfect, or as it should have been.
I lay by your side and watched the green of dawn
Climb over our bodies and bring out of darkness the one
Perfect face that made nothing else matter at all.

Not being a man of action

Lenin in Zurich given burnt oatmeal by his landlady:
"How lucky we are to have roast every day!"
Laughed, and went back to the Public Library;
dreams of action nourishing his exile.

A cottage in the middle of the wood.
Pipe and fire both drawing well;
even a glass of Teacher's whisky at my el-
bow . . .
Danton, Castro . . .
Men of action cannot flinch at blood.
I can though.

I know a company director who says
he'd kill anybody, he'll be bought
for a hundred thousand if he can't be caught.
He has the courage of our logic, which is money.
Whereas
the citizens of Rostov are very proud of
their new theatre
built in the shape of a tractor.
Each finds the other dangerous, and funny.

The kingcups burn like gas-jets by the lake.
Just before dark
blackcaps sang berserk behind the cottage.
At times, when I'm awake,
not half-asleep,
I'd like to go swimming, swimming, swimming in that lake,
but it's muddy, and nowhere more than three inches deep.

The delicate deer flick see-saw by to hide.
Up on the road at the top the huntsmen ride –
today the Hunt –
each heavily straddles his expense-account.

I live in this wood, like a marvellous green cage.
The bars are stationary, like trees:
outside are the slipping fields; I can go where I please.

O adder at my feet, your head
the size of my little finger-nail,
today I had to tread
on your neck, small as a cuticle,
watched your belly turn the colour of gun-metal.
O birds O flowers O snakes O fire-in-the-belly oatmeal
O Nelson cigarettes O Teacher's whisky
O daily daily daily
Daily Mail!
Killing hardly anything
I assert my triumphant uselessness, and sing,
while the auditioning stars on their cold blue xylophone go
          ting! ting! ting!

Satire I

for Patrick Creagh

My own John Patrick, since you'd like to know
    why did I leave my rich place at the court,
    or the nowadays version of it, where men go
(and you'd go too if asked, and so we ought)
    to make some money and to make a name
    innocently seeking to be sought
among the Wits, the Expenses and the Fame—
    I'll tell you what I know, as Wyatt told
    his friend John Poynz he'd given up the game,
gone back to Kent and Christendome and cold.
    Though Wyatt had a convention. He could say
    he didn't want their places and their gold,
not if his conscience was the price to pay;
    could leave out private reasons and moralise
    in the Palace versus Pastoral of his day.
While we, dear John, are too well taught the lies
    our super-ego tells us, to be sure
    quite what we're up to in our ego's eyes.
He knew this too of course, and knew the lure
    towards the chandeliers for the poet-moth,
    who wakes one day to find he can't endure
the trail of his monologue or the drone of his sloth
    one strophe longer, nor his fear he may
    have lost his sense and self-respect and both
will never cohabit again. He has to see
    if he exists at all outside his head
    (he knows he does some of the time, but you'll agree,
while living – it's sometimes splendid when he's dead –
    a poet's a burdensome, touchy thing to be).
    He goes there needing praises, love and bread

in just that order alas, and spoils all three
    by dragging with him the old chain and ball
    of his nagging other self: You think you're free
to take up masks and drop them: what if all
    your careful evasions, your meaningful standings-apart
    never meant anything but your own withdrawal?
Others commit their faces; you, by bat-light,
    a shadow at the window, *watch* the game.
    The sap in trees falls down as you recite
the one thousand variations on your name. –
    You see, John Patrick? I'm telling you why I went
    whereas Wyatt could take that for granted; but he'd the same
reasons I'm certain: a secular discontent
    with his divine one, and the brief illusion
    of a life more 'real' in London than in Kent.
You'll say the parallel's false, that television
    isn't today's equivalent of the court.
    'Your head's still on' you say. But the admiration,
the power, the cutting-a-figure-ness, the short
    shrift for those who weaken, the same nice
    distinctions between half-lies by men half-bought
that asken helpe of colours of devise
    to joyne the mene with eche extremitie,
    with the nerest vertue to cloke always the vise
(and thereby trivialise disastrously:)
    these not-quite-crooks, who care, and that's the worst
    I cannot, I. No, no, it will not be.
And not much to be proud of: at the first
    whiff of a compromise to up sticks and away
    hasn't much glamour about it, suggests a thirst
to be safer than sorry that we might call today
    by a harsher name, perhaps, than Wyatt knew.
    But I'll not bother to find one, though it may,
like nearly everything else, be nearly true.
    So many lives to live – so little time.
    Look – in these woods I've leisure to write to you.

Though ... what's the use if I should learn to climb
   into a still attention and my eyes
   go blunt as fingers pushing at old green
backdrops hung on hooks from plaster skies?
   This lake has less to offer than a bar.
   There isn't any point in telling lies
(you'd find me out if I did): these trees are far
   from substitute religion. Why pretend
   that most of the time they say much? But they are
(I watch them, as I write this, sway and bend,
   these beeches, their powdery trunks, less than half-way –
   this valley's, you know it, a hole under the wind,
it seldom reaches here – and the beeches' sway
   wastes itself at the top, the bole is still)
   they are – what? Presences? Undemanding? They
obscurely help me. Or perhaps they will.
   Pink buds begin, which seems a hopeful sign ...
   I am such an ordinary fool.

There's Pearse – *in Spaigne where oon must him inclyne*
   rather than to be, owtewerdly to seme:
   he shares our darkness, lights it up with wine;
let him who risks it be the first to blame.
   Fear of life – is that it? Shall we ever
   see proved our belief it's the opposite, learn to name
what swirls our darkness like a fish, the bright diver
   the under-sea mover in the imagination?
   Will it surface today, tomorrow (we're watching) and give a
hard, fast reason for a long obsession?
   So many lives to live, and none for long:
   times for watching, feeling for salvation.
Or will that fish by leaping prove us wrong,
   and fall back limply, by its fall convey
   there's only dark, and that's where fish belong?

Pearse, and you *where Christ is given in pray*
   for mony, poison and traison in Rome
   (only the method improved since Wyatt's day)
and I (for a while) in Gloucestershire, at home,
   eating court-earnings, bored with terza rhyme;
   where if thou list, John Patrick, for to come
thou shalt be judge how I do spend my time.

Diptyque touristque

1

The languorous isles, the tall bright-green bamboo;
the part of the plage where the girls run about toute nue
and the men oil themselves standing up hoping you're looking;
the helicopter at three o'clock, making
sure you're not doing whatever it is you're not meant to be
      doing.
The blackened young man dons his necklace and black chiffon
      shirt
and crimson trousers cut so tight they hurt.

The old girl with a young one at each horned foot scraping
and another two at her frizz of hair de-crêping
while she bulges, split apart, in her swimming suit:
the Salon de beauté, nine o'clock at night.

Every morning in the chic hotels
unsunburnt girls rinse out the lavatory bowls.
This is the perfect place, the perfect light;
Only for the altogether perfect could the price be right.

2

I resent having feet.
His feet, my feet, their feet; everyone has feet:
Feet – what a word! – all white
with shoes and crumpled up and useless.
If it was wings now . . . ah!
But perhaps there'd be hair under them;
and when I lifted them up
those around would receive the impression
also of how limited and ingloriously mortal
was the nature of my flight.

35

Goldie sapiens

When Goldie the golden eagle escaped from the Zoo
All the world went to Regents Park and we went too.
There he was, with an air of depression, a sooty hunch,
Digesting the grey-eyed merganser he had for lunch.
Under him children and coppers and mothers and fathers
And bare-kneed ornithologists with cameras
Hanging down to their ankles and lovers and others
Peeling damp cellophane from sandwiches stand and wait.
While running around in sad moustaches Keepers,
Hopelessly, like H. M. Bateman characters,
Shoo Pekes away from buckets of eagle bait.
Really, this bird was a National Occasion!
The Evening Standard published an hourly bulletin
As though it was getting in training for Sir Winston.
And none of us knew what we most wanted to see,
The Keepers allowed to go home or the bird to go free.
There was an appalling sense of a happy ending too –
Goldie was free but he kept an eye cocked on his Zoo.
Just then there started up where Goldie was,
A thrush fit to burst but we didn't listen because
We were enjoying the sight we'd come to see –
The only free eagle in captivity.
Later that evening the Nation breathed a sigh.
Goldie like us, Goldie the human and sage,
With tail between talons, had lallopped back to the cage.

May

Road-menders are flowers today, blooming in jeans,
Are men in the smoking advertisements, lolling in bright
    machines
That drip black shining tongues along the lanes
Shaded-in after with sweet white watered stones.
Beeches' leaves are fresh today, are peeled grapes stuck
On barbecue branches; bluebells broken on the deer-track
Hang in a thin blue vertigo after the deers' night-time feet;
    And May is behaving again, in the colours appropriate.

Though since the first summer that opened us something in May
Is delivered like milk and papers for someone who's gone away,
What's gone from us isn't May's fault and isn't our business.
Whatever we've left is ours and all there is:
As summer is, and so are we (for this one) who salute
Those rafts of other Mays drifting out of sight,
Road-menders and the roads they mend and deers' blue feet
    Dripping dead flowers out in the dark tonight.

No one

No one;
Only water, last year's leaves
And this year's, newly grown.

Walking alone.
Stumbling rather, through wet leaves
And fallen branches and marshes

Screened by beeches.
Following you, for why should you
Not be ahead of me here

As everywhere else you are?
No sounds; only the swish of my overcoat and water.
Nothing among the sunless stream-bed flora

Except a white-bibbed dipper
On a dripping branch
Ten feet away

Looking at me.
We both stand still, my nerve cracks first, I move,
The bird moves further.

Or rather
It guards the distance, keeping
The string between us taut.

And if I caught
Up with the bird what would I do with it?
Compress it like a silk scarf in my fist

And then, like silk released,
Explode it back to the air.
  Graveyard bluebells, water, bird and me.

  Still I can see
No sign of you who must have gone
  (You always do) the other way.

Deathday

The doctor in his surgery
tells the patient to undress
and fumbling with his underdrawers
rapes the patient quickly.
He's seen enough of faces
going blue before they're wheeled away
to know to catch the flesh still warm,
his and theirs, you have to hurry.
That accomplished, at his table,
under the shaded table lamp,
approves the moisture of his fingers' ends,
sighs and from the hat-rack takes his hat
to feel its roundness rounding round his head,
to walk down shine-green corridors of sweat
he runs his fingers through –
always physical, absent-minded, leaving his mark.
Outside, the early editions of people and papers
go soggy in air, go glup and glup
down gratings, irretrievably over.
While, everywhere, hidden, in surprising places,
are those who from the inside of their heads
have hanging on a string a pendulum
that swings tick-tock, and never hurries.
Their eyes are deep as skies, go down
to the connected place – their faces,
carved like soap-stone, stem the waters.
These under oxygen when they die
are loud as radios as they're wheeled away.
These, with a stone's
patience, who have waited out
their drying season.

What is surprising is that not everyone's
only ambition in the world is
to be like them, and to love their tired eyes.

Closing Down

(for K.K.)

Sometimes my whole being
  itches like a bird-table
lousy with starlings.

You itched all over.
  I would say 'Keep still'
myself jumping like a cracker.

How we got like that I do not know.
  You, Dionysus,
casting me for Apollo.

Me, posing as the settled one.
  You, married and three children;
puzzled by this.

So we fought;
  a blurted duologue of itching;
sharing that.

But you were an actor resenting the part he is given.
You only half-learned yours; and always
answered a door you didn't approve of and who
the hell dared knock at it anyway – '*You?*'
To understand, (I understood, as in a mirror)
is to forgive . . . some things. Not enough.
My only, and entirely, my brother.

Sometimes when I drove away
I saw you in the mirror
watching after me
standing in the street.
If I'd have turned
you would have feigned
indifference like a cat.

Coughing up cigarette butts
like gall-stones
drinking quick ones
quicker, pulling fast ones
faster, loss of self-respect
you had the courage
to acknowledge.
Even your self-pity
crocodile tears.
So, in the middle years,
although of course defeated
you were never gelded
by the city.

You were too human
to be good and too
good for your own.
And though it is true we never
talked perfectly or well
because I live I still
call on a wave-band
pitched only for you
which only you could hear;
each, in dumbness, the other.

Now no one hears a sound.
My only, and entirely my brother.

"This philosophy"
   said Goethe,
"if what the Englishman tells us
   is true,
has nothing foreign;
   on the contrary,
the epochs through which we all pass
   are repeated in it.
When we are children
   we are sensualists;
idealists when we love,
   and attribute
to the beloved object
   qualities which she does not
naturally possess."
   (She might though, mightn't she,
naturally?)
   "Love wavers,"
(it does, yes)
   "we doubt her fidelity"
(the truth of our mutual feelings)
   "and are sceptics
before we think of it.
   The rest of life is indifferent;
we let it go as it will,
   and end,"
(so that's it,
   so that's what's coming on!
But, dear Heaven, he was nearly eighty!)
   "like the Indian
philosopher, in quietism."

Birthday

It's raining today, a dark rain,
On water and breaking trees. It's cold.
A day for dying and answering questions on.
Only a few dark days like this
I'm half-way through, I'm thirty-five years old.

And if I should die this minute – supposing –
Looking at nothing much, the wall
Between me, the lamp, and the coughing hillside,
How surprised would I be to snap off
Like a twig and go suddenly flying? Hardly at all.

You? With all your sins
Sticking like merde in your hair? And everyone
(Think how many you know already)
Who's got there before you waving like mad
And calling hallo like a wartime railway station?

Something like that. At least for a while.
Things fall away. We might go on –
Speak in a language of poppies and roses
With faces we love. There may be one
Or two we knew as deep as that, or one –

Who takes us and teaches us, and after,
So mixed up together we no longer care
Which is ourself or the other, go flying
As free and as one as a light flash, the fusion
Quick or as long, as irrelevant as a light-year.

It's pretty scary. But what is a soul
If not a big wish in a small fool
If we have one at all? One or two things
Suggest we may. But no more than you
Can I tell today if yesterday's message was true.

And not all of us soon, and none of us surely
Make for the light. It may depend
How thick our eyes go blind in the dazzle
After how deep and dark we dug
A frozen hole we fell through in the end.

The walls are shaking . . . The wind like an Irish
Country portent laughs in the rigging
Of coffin trees pretending it's crying.
Only a few dark days like this
To think how to climb from the hole these days are digging.

Surviving

I am oh, I am sick
oh, heartily, I am sick of grief
that's round me like a collar on a thief,
bending my neck
into an angle, wounded, weak,
an impermissably apologetic back.

I count the towels we shared. They wear.
Burn them. Move on. Move on where?
Move on as usual, wearing the new collar?
('Rag and bone' a street man calls outside the cellar
where your dresses are . . . No one survives.
You are not the first of my two wives.

Time is not sequence.) Could I incorporate
our grief (no one ever has, we shriek
and bend the neck or turn our back
or die) if I could learn to bear
grief (and not the stupid collar that I wear)
then might we, both together, celebrate.

And Odysseus wept

Pink nightdresses in pink, night, boutique windows
And every sweet elegant dream such things give rise to –
Why should I hate them, I've not been deprived of them?

Soft murmurs of terraces, lime trees and lapping of water;
Slim-ankled Ino, her eyes in the lamplight like water.
Why did they look at me, who had never dared pray for them?

The pride of attractiveness burns inside their faces,
Those who wear like togas their successes.
Why should I envy them, who have also won them?

Apartments where all is clarity – bathrooms smell
Of powdered skin, and sponges, and Chanel –
Why should I scoff, I who have thanked God for them?

The truth of love, perfections, visions, dreams,
A face in the morning, joy falling like coins –
Why should I bark at these, I who have counted them?

I, with the heart of a lover, heart of a hater,
Who have taken nothing easy since the day I was born,
Why should I hate the things I've taken, who have paid for them?

The girl in the bar who asks for a table for one,
A little crazy perhaps, but lovely, her hair hanging down,
Bypasses me and sits (I'm exact) with a cross-eyed Italian.

I don't even mind she misses out me, perhaps I prefer to watch
    them?
I have lived in the waves of the sea, tossed up, borne down.
Why should I weep at the waves, that have saved me and wrecked
    me so often?

Piazza di Spagna

Moving

There is a perfect
socket at the centre
in whose groove
our lives would move
                    effortlessly.
Some physical men
have sometimes found it;
great games-players
on their day:
Garfield Sobers;
what do the others
find so difficult?
See, his simpleness!

In happiness
I spread my arms.
Dark
fish move in their shadow.

And I rejoice
my life as it should be –
moving towards
                    effortfully
its centre –
a kind of
happy nightmare.

1966